CHINESE STORIES
FOUR MAJOR CONTRIBUTIONS

Tea

Edited by Li Chaodong

Illustrated by Zhang Weilai

Translated by Daniel Jingyuan Ni and Joanna Jiayan Zhang

Books Beyond Boundaries

ROYAL COLLINS

Hundreds of years ago, at Qinghebao in Benxi, Liaoning, two armies stood in strict battle arrays, ready for conflict. It is hard to imagine that what sparked this war was a mere handful of tea leaves.

At that time, the Ming Dynasty (AD 1368–1644) had suspended the supply of tea to the Mongols and various Manchu tribes. To obtain the tea that was essential to their daily lives, the Mongols and Manchus launched the "Battle of Qinghebao." This war lasted for three years and caused immense casualties on both sides.

Today, thanks to modern transportation and free trade, everyone can enjoy tea anytime, anywhere, whether in the north or the south.

But why is tea, which doesn't fill the stomach, considered as essential as firewood, rice, oil, salt, soy sauce, and vinegar in the traditional Chinese saying: "Firewood, rice, oil, salt, soy sauce, vinegar, and tea"? Let's explore.

China is the birthplace of tea. Tea plants thrive in warm, humid, and shaded environments and first appeared in southwestern China, particularly in Sichuan and Yunnan provinces.

In ancient times, tea leaves were used as medicine to detoxify. Legend has it that Shennong, the mythical figure who tasted hundreds of herbs, was poisoned and cured himself by chewing tea leaves.

By the Tang and Song dynasties, tea had become a staple food ingredient with many pairings.

Later, people began to boil tea leaves with other ingredients to make "tea porridge."

As the Qin Dynasty (221–206 BC) unified China, tea spread eastward from the Bashu region (modern-day Sichuan and Chongqing) along the Yangtze River.

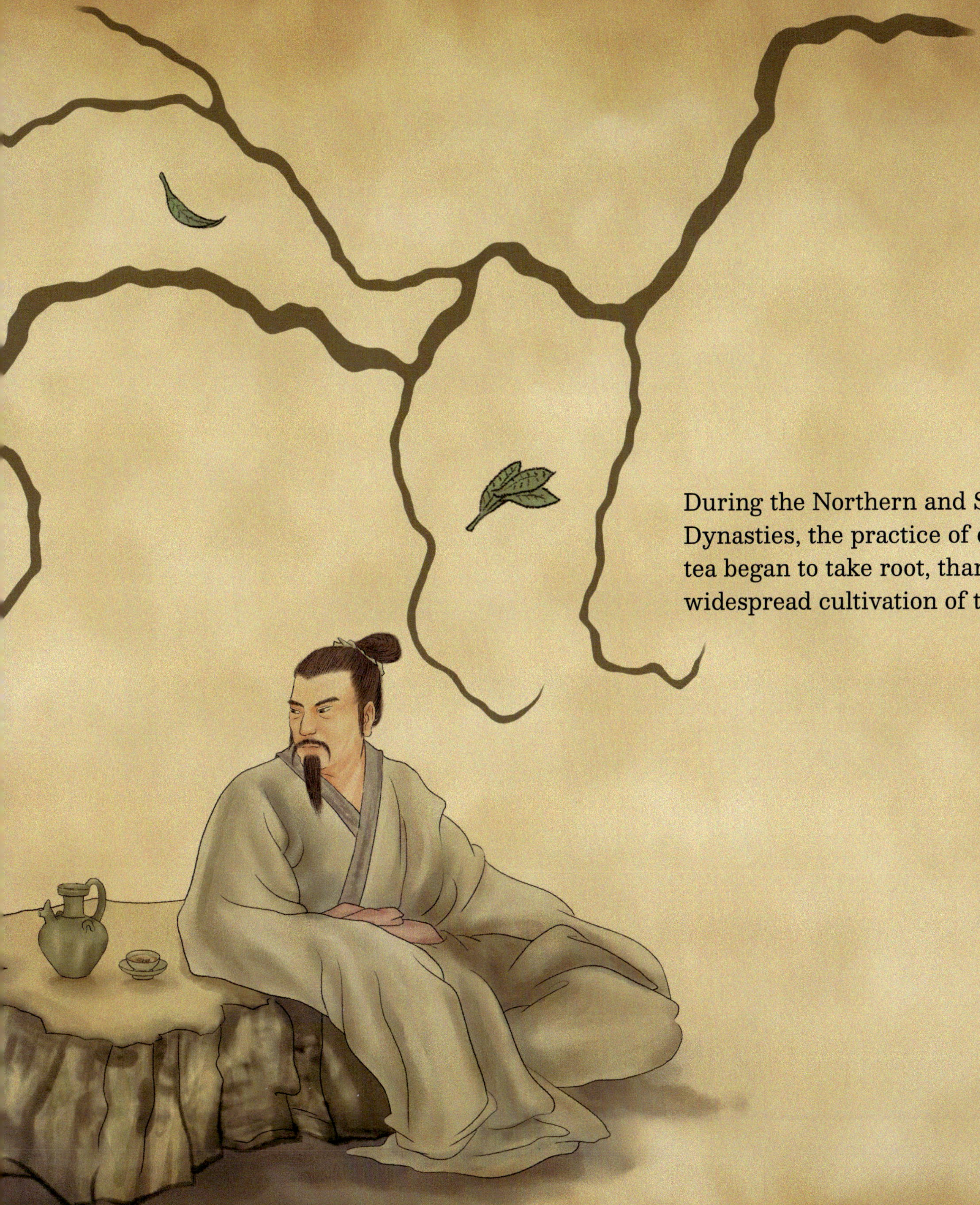

During the Northern and Southern Dynasties, the practice of drinking tea began to take root, thanks to the widespread cultivation of tea plants.

By the Tang Dynasty (AD 618–907), tea had become a household drink, in part due to Buddhism's popularity.

Buddhist monks embraced tea as a substitute for alcohol, which was prohibited in monasteries. Tea helped them stay awake and meditate. In southern temples, it became common practice for monks to drink tea.

One of the most famous figures in tea history, "Tea Saint" Lu Yu, lived during this time.

Adopted by a Buddhist abbot, Lu Yu became fascinated with tea culture.

He traveled to tea-growing regions across China and wrote *The Book of Tea*, the first comprehensive work on tea culture.

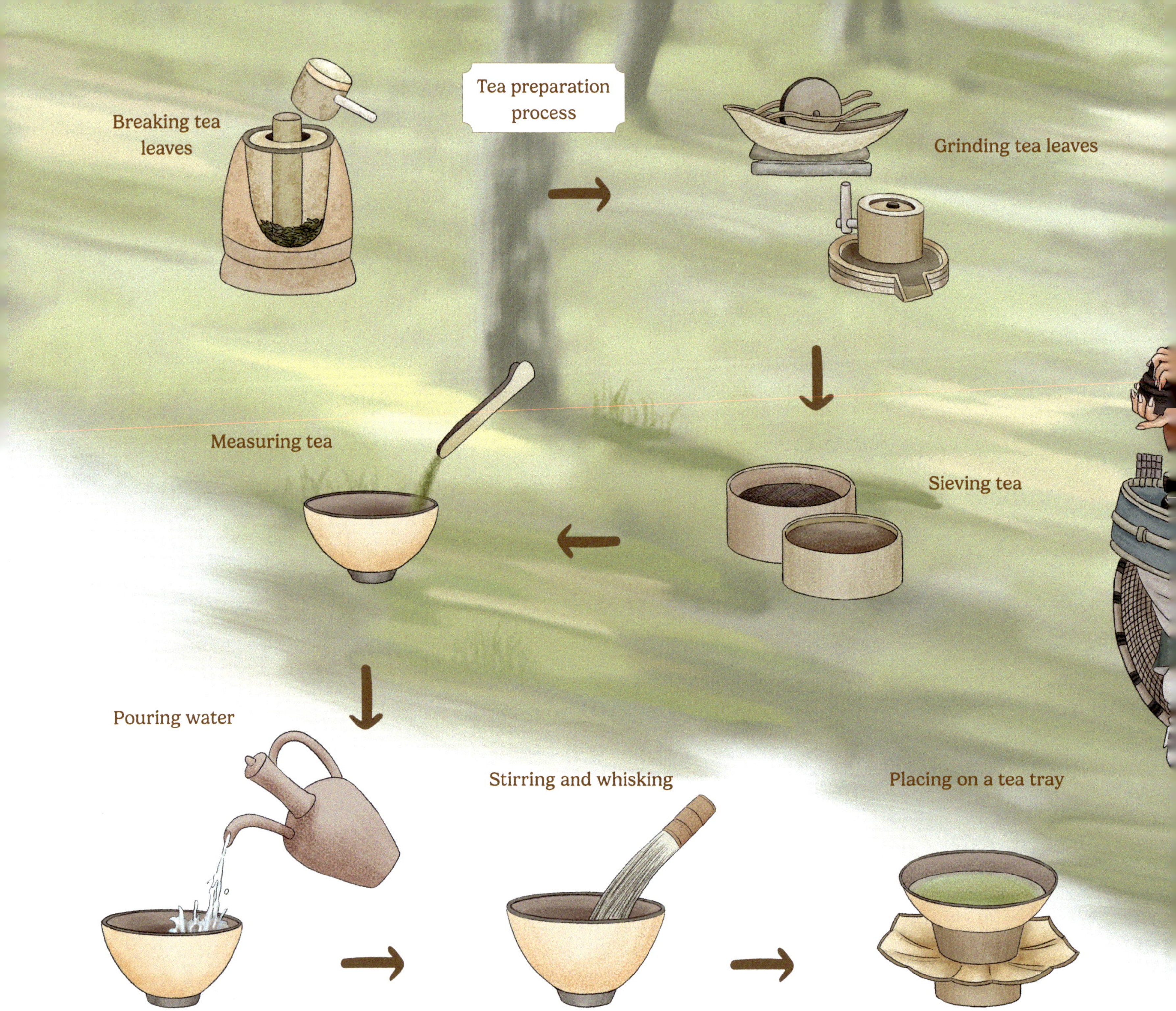

China's climate shifted during the Song Dynasty (AD 960–1279), leading to colder weather. In Fujian, where the climate remained relatively mild and the soil was perfect for tea cultivation, tea trees sprouted earlier than in other regions. This made southern Fujian a key center for tea production.

During this period, tea culture flourished. People developed new ways to enjoy tea, including "tea preparation," "tea competitions," and "tea sharing." These practices continued through the Ming and Qing dynasties, showcasing the creativity and communal spirit of tea enthusiasts.

In the Tang Dynasty, Japanese monks brought tea tree seeds back to Japan, laying the foundation for Japan's tea culture.

The Japanese adapted Chinese tea preparation methods into their own unique matcha tea ceremony.

Tea hundred performances (a traditional folk art where patterns and images are formed on the surface of tea broth)

和敬清寂

Today, various regions have developed distinct tea-drinking customs.

Kunming's nine-course tea ceremony

People in Guangzhou enjoy morning tea

Chaoshan Kung Fu tea
Northern-style large bowl tea
Chengdu's covered bowl tea

The custom of drinking tea in the Central Plains quickly spread to the border regions, where the local diet was predominantly beef and mutton, with limited access to fruits and vegetables. This dietary imbalance often led to poor gastrointestinal health. Tea, known for aiding digestion and relieving indigestion, became highly valued and was revered as the "tea of life" by the people in these areas. However, since the border regions did not produce tea, all supplies were transported from the Central Plains.

Tea from Sichuan and Yunnan was carried to Xizang, where it was exchanged by people in Xizang for fur, horses, and other goods. In the rugged mountain valleys, caravans of traders traversed challenging terrain, forming the vibrant and bustling "Tea-Horse Road."

People in Xizang love to drink butter tea.

❶ Place tea leaves in a pot with water and boil until a thick broth forms.

❷ Strain the tea leaves and discard them.

❸ Pour the tea broth into a tea churn, add butter and salt, and churn repeatedly to blend the butter with the tea.

Butter helps ward off the cold, while tea reduces greasiness and aids digestion. For these reasons, people in Xizang enjoy butter tea with every meal.

5 And just like that, butter tea is ready.

4 Pour the mixture back into the pot and heat it again.

Tea was introduced to Xinjiang through the Silk Road, which served as a vital trade route not only for silk but also for tea and porcelain.

In contrast, the residents of southern Xinjiang, who live in oasis areas and primarily engage in farming, enjoy fragrant fruits and vegetables. When drinking tea, they prefer to add a variety of spices to create spiced tea, which they often pair with baked *nang* bread.

In northern Xinjiang, between the Altay Mountains and the Tianshan Mountains, expansive pastures dominate the landscape. The people here often use local ingredients to make milk tea, blending tea with goat's milk or cow's milk for a rich and creamy beverage.

Mongolians have a deep fondness for salty milk tea. Early each morning, they break up brick tea and boil it in water, then add milk and salt to create their signature beverage. They enjoy this tea alongside fried rice, keeping any leftovers simmering on a low flame to ensure it stays warm and readily available throughout the day.

The once brutal "Battle of Qinghebao" is now a distant memory. Today, even in Inner Mongolia, tea is easily accessible to meet the daily needs of the people.

Tea has not only shaped the lives of ethnic minorities but has also made its way to foreign countries.

In the 17th century, as the Russian nation around the Moscow region was forming and rapidly expanding eastward, Mongolia maintained commercial exchanges with Russia.

During this period, the Mongolian khan presented tea to the czar, marking the first introduction of tea to Russia. However, it initially failed to capture widespread interest.

During the Qing Dynasty (AD 1616–1911), as Russian influence extended into Heilongjiang, the czar sent envoys to China seeking direct trade. These envoys frequently returned to Russia with tea as gifts. Over time, tea began to gain popularity, especially among the Russian aristocracy, laying the foundation for its enduring cultural significance in Russia.

The Russian aristocracy's growing appreciation and enthusiasm for tea significantly boosted the development of the Sino-Russian tea trade. Following several small-scale conflicts, the two nations established peaceful relations, ushering in an era of unprecedented trade prosperity.

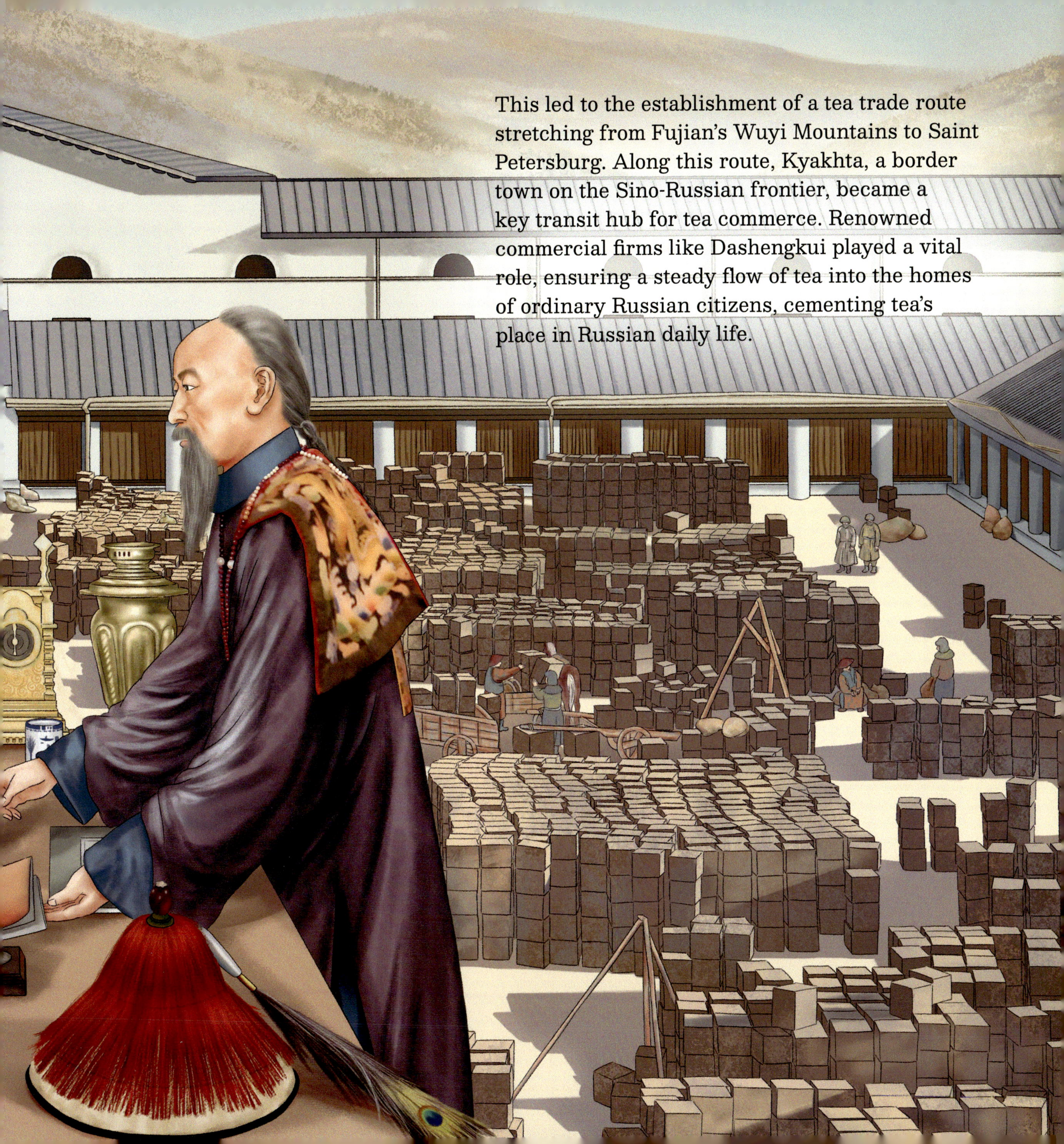

This led to the establishment of a tea trade route stretching from Fujian's Wuyi Mountains to Saint Petersburg. Along this route, Kyakhta, a border town on the Sino-Russian frontier, became a key transit hub for tea commerce. Renowned commercial firms like Dashengkui played a vital role, ensuring a steady flow of tea into the homes of ordinary Russian citizens, cementing tea's place in Russian daily life.

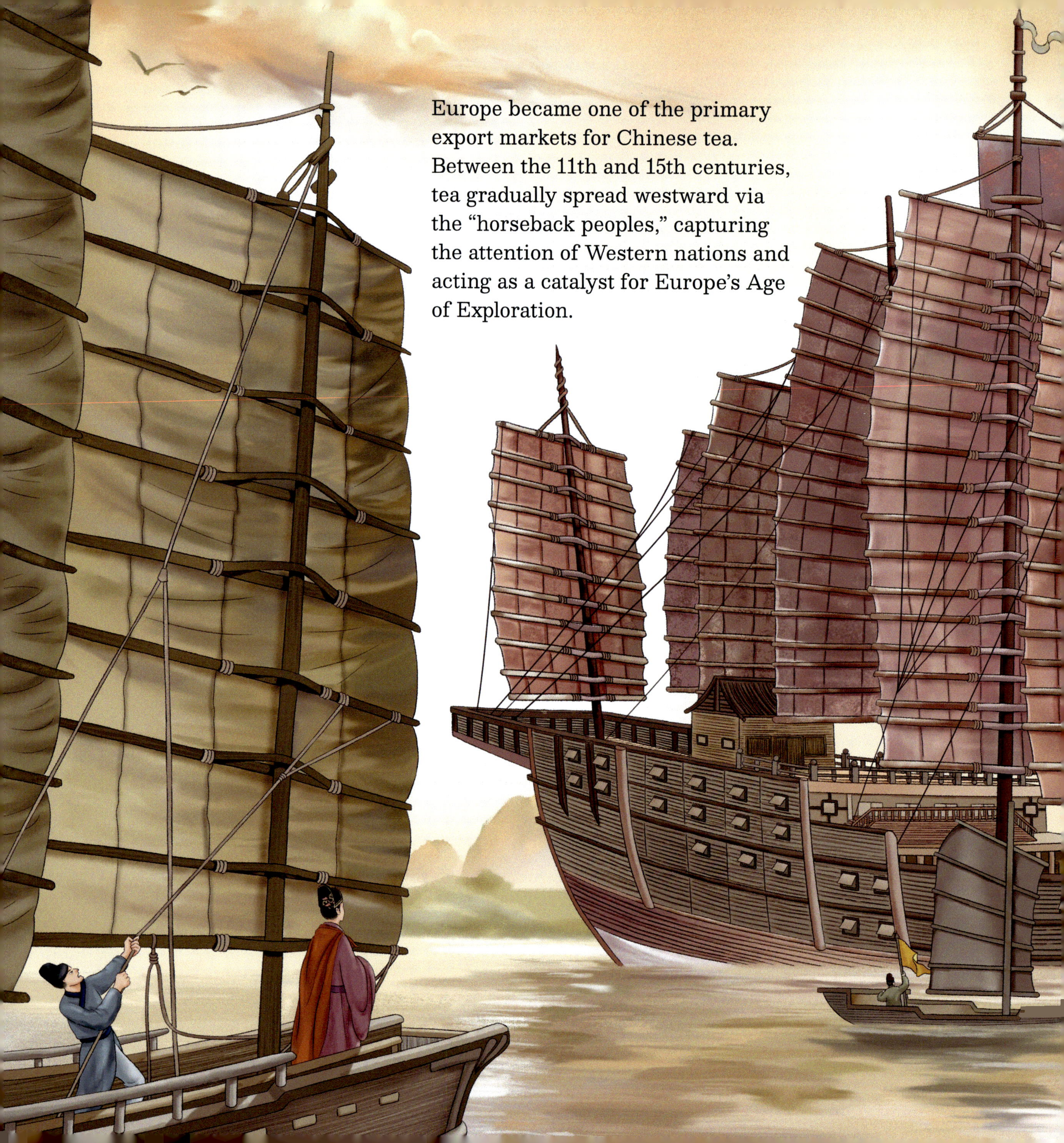

Europe became one of the primary export markets for Chinese tea. Between the 11th and 15th centuries, tea gradually spread westward via the "horseback peoples," capturing the attention of Western nations and acting as a catalyst for Europe's Age of Exploration.

Following the discovery of new sea routes, ships from Spain, Portugal, the Netherlands, and Britain transported tea to Europe, profoundly transforming the daily lives and cultural practices of its people.

The British fell in love with tea at first sip. However, the long sea journey meant that ships often took more than six months to deliver tea to Britain. The sea's moisture caused the tea to ferment, resulting in an unpleasant taste. To counter this, the British added milk, sugar, and lemon—a practice that endures to this day.

Afternoon tea became a cherished tradition among the British aristocracy. A popular folk song captures this sentiment: "When the clock strikes four, everything in the world stops for tea." Even during wartime, the British faithfully upheld their afternoon tea ritual.

TEA
TEA

Trade brought with it taxation. By the mid-to-late Tang Dynasty, the government began taxing the tea trade. From that period through the Qing Dynasty, tea taxes ranked alongside salt and iron as one of the most important revenue sources.

Tea was not only a source of wealth but also a unique product of China, serving as a cornerstone for the nation's interactions with other cultures.

In the 18th century, as the tea trade expanded, China closely guarded the origins of tea and restricted foreign merchants to trading at the “Thirteen Factories of Canton.” Payment was accepted only in gold and silver, ensuring the trade remained advantageous to China.

Chinese tea merchants organized into guilds known as "hometown associations," which, along with the Thirteen Factories of Canton, firmly controlled the domestic and foreign tea markets. This monopoly led to the emergence of wealthy and influential tea merchants.

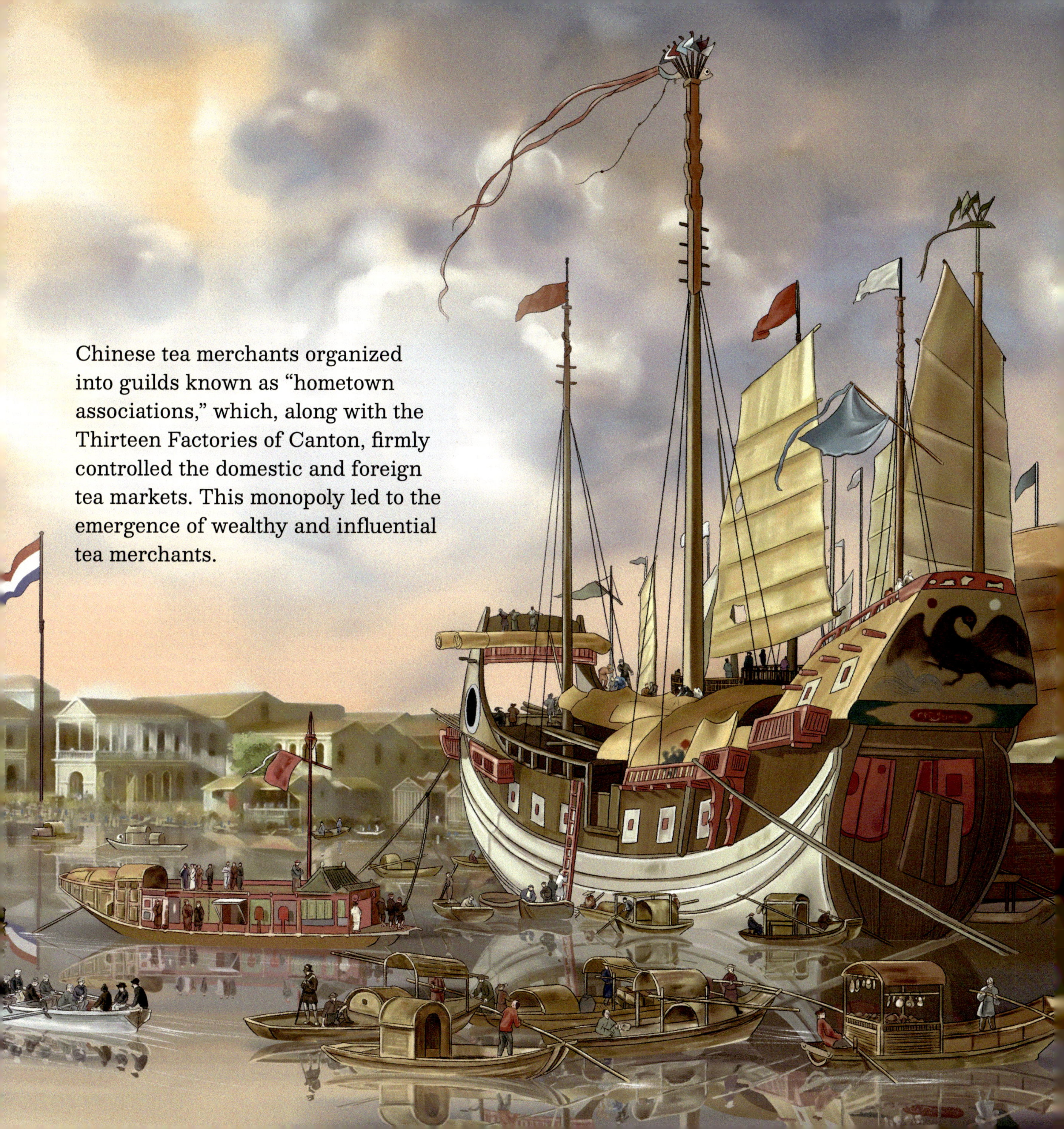

As Europe's demand for tea grew, Britain sought ways to reduce its dependence on Chinese tea.

The British eventually acquired Chinese tea seeds and hired Chinese workers to cultivate tea in India. Today, black tea from India and Sri Lanka has gained global popularity and is exported worldwide.

In the 18th century, North America, still under European colonial rule, also developed a love for tea. Britain's East India Company monopolized Chinese tea sales, profiting by selling it at inflated prices.

In 1773, Britain banned private tea trade in North America to offload surplus tea stored by the East India Company. This sparked outrage among locals, culminating in the Boston Tea Party, where large amounts of tea were dumped into the sea. This act became a key trigger for the American Revolutionary War.

Despite its monopoly on the Chinese tea trade, Britain faced a persistent issue: China's self-sufficiency meant British goods found little market there, while Chinese tea and other goods were highly sought after abroad.

To purchase tea and other Chinese products, Britain paid vast amounts of silver, creating a "one-way flow" of silver into China. Unable to profit from conventional trade, Britain turned to sell opium, an addictive substance.

In response, the Qing government implemented opium bans, with Lin Zexu famously destroying opium at Humen. This act infringed on British interests, leading to the Opium War. This conflict marked the beginning of a disastrous era in modern Chinese history.

Today, tea is enjoyed in over 100 countries and regions, becoming a universal social tradition. Tea drinking connects people worldwide, fostering cultural exchange and contributing to global development.

hite Tea
Green Tea
ellow Tea
Oolong Tea
Black Tea
Dark Tea

Delicious tea leaves owe their flavor to the complex tea-making process.

Planting

Fixing

Rolling

Picking
Withering
Drying

Chinese Stories: Four Major Contributions

Tea

Edited by Li Chaodong
Illustrated by Zhang Weilai
Translated by Daniel Jingyuan Ni and Joanna Jiayan Zhang

First published in 2024 by Royal Collins Publishing Group Inc.
Groupe Publication Royal Collins Inc.
550-555 boul. René-Lévesque O Montréal (Québec) H2Z1B1 Canada

10 9 8 7 6 5 4 3 2 1

ISBN: 978-1-4878-1330-7

To find out more about our publications, please visit www.royalcollins.com.

About the Editor

LI CHAODONG, born in 1963, is a prominent figure in China's education publishing industry and a graduate of the Department of History at East China Normal University. Over his distinguished career, he has edited and published more than 50 book series. He has been honored as a "National Leading Talent in Press and Publication" and recognized as "China's Annual Publication Figure." Li currently serves as the Founding Vice President of the All-China Federation of Industry and Commerce Book Industry Chamber of Commerce, Vice President of the Fifth Council of the China Book Publishing Association, and Vice Chairman of both the Anhui and Jiangsu Publishing Associations.